FIRST IMPRESSIONS

JUV
ND
553
.M7
W24
1991

Waldron, Ann.

Claude Monet.

$19.95

DATE	BORROWER'S NAME		
JUN 2 3 1997	DEC 0 6 1999		
JUN 1 2 1998	JAN 1 9 2001		
	FEB 2 7 2001		
DEC 2 1 1998			
JAN 0 8 1999	JUL 2 6 2001		
	FEB - 1 2003		
FEB 1 0 1999			
MAR 2 6 1999	FEB 2 1 2003		
APR 1 4 1999			
JUN 0 1 1999	AUG 2 4 2004		
	MAY 0 5 2005		
OCT 2 5 1999			
NOV 1 5 1999			

BAKER & TAYLOR   003294 9537668   TAYLOR

Claude Monet 72

Ann Waldron

Claude Monet

First Impressions

HARRY N. ABRAMS, INC.

PUBLISHERS

NEW YORK

SERIES EDITOR: Robert Morton
EDITOR: Ellyn Childs Allison
DESIGNER: Joan Lockhart
PHOTO RESEARCH: Barbara Lyons

LIBRARY OF CONGRESS CATALOGING-IN-PUBLICATION DATA

Waldron, Ann.
    Claude Monet / Ann Waldron.
        p.   cm. — (First impressions)
    Includes index.
    Summary: Examines the life and work of Monet, describing his struggle
for artistic recognition and providing examples of his paintings.
    ISBN 0–8109–3620–8 (cloth)
    1. Monet, Claude, 1840–1926—Juvenile literature.   2. Painters—
France—Biography—Juvenile literature.   3. Impressionism (Art)—
France—Juvenile literature.   [1. Monet, Claude, 1840–1926.
2. Artists.   3. Painting, French.   4. Painting, Modern—19th
century—France.   5. Art appreciation.]   I. Title.   II. Series.
ND553.M7W24   1991
759.4—dc20
[B]   91–8602
                                                            CIP

Claude Monet

I

"I WOULD BE A PAINTER"

At sixteen, Claude Monet was already famous in Le Havre, the French port city where he lived. For years he had been drawing cartoons of his teachers at school and giving them to his friends. He sold other caricatures to people who asked for them. Demand for his drawings grew until he was getting 20 francs (about $60 today) for each picture. "If I had continued, I would be a millionaire," Monet said when he was an old man.

Monet did more than a hundred caricatures at this price and gave the money to his aunt for safekeeping. Every Sunday he took fresh drawings down to the art-supply store in the Rue de Paris, the main street in Le Havre, where the proprietor framed them and hung them in the window. Young Monet would walk past the shop for the sheer joy of seeing people admire his work. "I almost burst out of my skin with pride," he said.

The proprietor of the store liked the tall, sturdy teenager, with olive skin, bright dark eyes, and long dark hair brushed back from his face. Several times he told him that Monet should meet Eugène Boudin, whose paintings of the sea and beaches near Le Havre hung in the window beside Monet's caricatures. "He studied in Paris. He knows his craft, he could give you some good advice," the proprietor said. Like most people in Le Havre, however, Monet did not care for Boudin's little pictures. He also thought Boudin was mad because he lived like a

A fellow student painted this portrait of Monet
at the age of eighteen.

When he was about sixteen Monet drew this caricature, perhaps a merchant or city official of Le Havre. Using charcoal for the black lines and adding touches of brown, pink, and white chalk, the young artist made a convincing likeness, but exaggerated the cigar.

tramp, slept wherever he could, and used the money he got from his pictures—which he often sold for only a franc apiece—to buy more paints and canvases.

Once Boudin and Monet happened to be in the shop at the same time and the proprietor introduced them. Boudin complimented Monet on his caricatures. "They're amusing, clever, and spirited," he said. "But you're not going to stop there, I hope. Study, learn to see and to paint—do landscapes."

Monet was not won over by the older man. When Boudin invited Monet to paint landscapes with him in the open air, the boy refused. Finally, one summer day, Monet decided to give it a try. He bought some tubes of oil paint and set out with Boudin. They walked to Rouelles, two miles from Le Havre. Monet set up his easel and began to daub his canvas. Then he watched Boudin paint. It was a revelation to watch the older man slowly capture on canvas the precise look and feel of the sky and the landscape.

"Suddenly, it was as though a veil had been ripped from my eyes,"

Monet later said. "I understood, I saw, what painting could be! From that moment on, my way was clear, my destiny decreed. I would be a painter, no matter what. And I understood nature and I learned at the same time to love it." Working beside Boudin had taught him an important lesson: "Everything that's painted directly on the spot always has much more strength and power and life than anything that's done later in the studio."

Monet had been born in Paris on November 14, 1840. Named Oscar-Claude (he later dropped the Oscar), he was the second son of Adolphe and Louise-Justine Monet. His parents lived in an apartment above the family grocery store. When Claude was about five, Marie-Jeanne Lecadre, his aunt, suggested that Adolphe join her husband in a wholesale grocery business that supplied the ships at the docks in Le Havre. So Claude, with his older brother, Léon, and their parents, moved to Le Havre, the largest port in France, a city of shipowners and international merchants who did business all over the world. For an observant boy, the maze of docks and jetties, piled high with mahogany logs, dates, and bags of sugar and coffee beans, was a heaven of sights

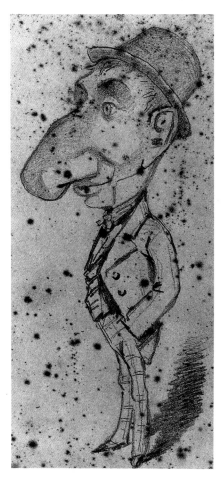

In another cartoon portrait Monet focused on his subject's facial features to poke some fun at him.

and sounds and smells. Rowboats crossed the bay to Honfleur and tall sailing ships moved out to sea, bound for Algiers, New Orleans, India, and Africa.

Claude went to a small private school and then, when he was eleven, to a kind of high school called the Collège du Havre, attended by about two hundred students. The other pupils liked Monet, who was good-natured, exuberant, and not interested in any of his studies except drawing.

Classes lasted two hours in the morning and two hours in the afternoon. Monet drew a great deal of the time, mostly in the margins of his schoolbooks and notebooks. Using both pencil and pen, he drew fantastic animals as well as cruel caricatures of his teachers. In addition to cartoons, he made sketches of people, landscapes, and boats, for the harbor was only a few blocks from the school.

Monet's drawing teacher was François-Charles Ochard, a bald-headed, red-faced man with a fine white beard, who had taught at the school for twenty years and would remain another twenty. Ochard had studied under Jacques-Louis David, France's most influential painter earlier in the century, and had had paintings accepted for display on three different occasions at the great exhibition in Paris called the Salon. He taught art the way it was taught all over France: first, his

Le Havre's beaches, waterfront, and active harbor offered Monet many subjects for drawings. Boats and the sea became lifelong favorites of his.

students learned to draw the human form from plaster casts of ancient Greek and Roman statues; after years of that, they were allowed to draw living models. Eventually, they might learn to paint.

Monet stayed at the Collège du Havre until at least January 1857, when his mother died. Shortly thereafter, his uncle Jacques also died and Claude, Léon, and their father moved in with Madame Lecadre. She was an amateur painter herself and knew many professional artists. Having no children of her own, she took a special interest in Claude and his drawing. While his father did not encourage Monet to become an artist, his aunt did. She let him use her studio and insisted that he continue to work at his drawing.

Boudin was his first real teacher. The two friends painted together for several months. A landscape view of a small valley with a brook—a painting that Monet did when he was seventeen called *A View Taken at Rouelles*—was hung in the municipal exhibition in Le Havre in August–September 1858. Boudin had two landscapes in the same exhibition.

Boudin's insistence on painting landscapes and for working on them outdoors went against the current of fashion, as did his habit of painting ordinary people wearing ordinary clothes. Successful artists chose serious and educational subjects from French history, such as *The Death of the Duke of Guise,* which shows the assassination of a nobleman three hundred years before by men shown in the costume of the time — tights, ruffs, capes, and swords. Or they might choose a subject from Greek or Roman mythology, like "Mars Disarmed by Venus and the Three Graces," in which a nude Venus crowns Mars, the Roman god of war, with a wreath of flowers. There was nothing in these pictures that reflected contemporary life. They were painted in studios, with models wearing costumes and posing as they thought dukes and Greek gods should look. What is more, painters used mostly dark colors, which were supposed to reflect the *seriousness* of the subject and of the noble art of painting.

Some painters did landscapes, but no one in the French art world at the time considered this work as important as historical or mythological pictures. Art schools did not even teach landscape painting. Teachers admitted that quick sketches made out-of-doors could be valuable, but they insisted that the artists should bring these sketches back to the studio and complete them there. They were to edit the details, refine the colors, and finish them with a surface so smooth that the marks of the brushstrokes were invisible.

Monet had heard about the Paris art world, and by the time he was eighteen he was eager to leave Le Havre and to see the great capital and the work that painters were doing there. Boudin had received a grant to study art in Paris, and in August 1858, Adolphe Monet applied to the city council for a similar grant for Claude. But before the council acted on the request, in April 1859, young Monet had already left.

With an allowance from his father in his pocket, Monet arrived in Paris in time to see the paintings in the Salon. He must have been dazzled, for the Salon was held in the huge glass-roofed exhibition hall called the Palais de l'Industrie on the Champs-Elysées, in the center of the city. More than two thousand paintings hung on the walls and thousands of people visited each day. All artists wanted to have their work accepted for exhibition at the Salon; it was the only way to win recognition and prizes and the best way to find buyers. But the judges who decided which pictures would hang in the Salon were painters and teachers who admired the traditional ways of painting.

Art schools of Monet's day offered young artists a chance to draw nude models so they could better understand the human body and learn how to portray it accurately. When a model wasn't available they would draw from plaster casts of ancient Greek and Roman statues.

With a cape slung over his shoulders,
eighteen-year-old Monet struck a dashing
pose for this photograph.

Monet wrote to Boudin with excitement about some of the pictures he had admired, among them the work of two landscape painters — Constant Troyon and Charles-François Daubigny. He called on Troyon, a painter who knew Boudin, and showed him two of his paintings. Troyon told Claude he had a good sense of color but that he had done easy things. If he wanted to be a serious artist, he should enter an academy where he could learn to draw the figure. Monet must draw a great deal, Troyon said, but still he must not neglect painting and from time to time he should go and work in the country. Troyon encouraged him: "Show me what you do. Be serious about art. You will succeed." That was all Monet needed to hear.

In May 1859, the city council of Le Havre voted to deny Monet's request for a grant, and Adolphe ordered him home. Claude said he would stay in Paris. His father said, "You'll get no money from me."

"I'll get by," Claude said. He had money of his own—the 2,000 francs from his caricatures that his aunt had saved for him—and in Paris a young man could live on a few francs a month. He moved out of the hotel where he had been staying and rented a room on the Place Pigalle, not too far from the Rue Laffitte, where he was born. The neighborhood was full of artists' studios and cafés where painters and poets flocked.

As for his art education, Monet's family and Troyon advised him to study with Thomas Couture, a respected artist and a teacher at the official French art school, the Ecole des Beaux-Arts. Couture, who had just written a textbook on painting, had triumphed at the Salon twelve years before with *Romans of the Decadence*, a huge picture twenty-five feet wide by fifteen feet high. The painting, which shows half-dressed men and women drinking and reclining in a splendid classical banquet setting, was intended to teach the moral lesson that debauchery and dissipation had sapped the strength of the Romans. It was just the kind of thing—an imaginary historical scene in which posed models were given a false grandeur—that Monet was learning

1847

Thomas Couture. ROMANS OF THE DECADENCE

Couture's painting, shown at the Salon of 1847, gave Parisians a little reminder of ancient history and a good chance to look at unclothed human bodies without feeling naughty.

to scorn. Furthermore, Monet disliked Couture personally.

So, instead of trying to study with Couture at the Ecole des Beaux-Arts, Monet chose the Académie Suisse, run by a man who had been a painter's model and whom the students called Père (Father) Suisse. It

was one of the free studios in Paris where artists could chip in to pay for a model and work without advice and criticism from a teacher.

The Académie Suisse was on the second floor of a building on a small island called the Ile de la Cité in the Seine River, which runs through Paris. At the top of the stairs, the door on the left opened into the office of a dentist, whose patients sometimes got lost and confronted a nude model in the Académie Suisse, which was reached through the right-hand door. The studio opened early every morning and stayed open until ten o'clock at night. The young painters chatted and joked while they worked. Unlike traditional studios, where students drew plaster casts of classical sculptures for years before they drew a live model, the Académie Suisse was a relaxed place. The students could use a pencil, a brush, or a palette knife, work in watercolor or oil, paint a still life or work from the model. Monet diligently practiced his drawing.

At the Académie Suisse, Monet made friends with Camille Pissarro, a student ten years older than himself. Pissarro was the son of a well-to-do family on the island of St. Thomas in the Danish West Indies. He had realized he did not want to work in his father's business and ran away from home. But his father was tolerant; if he was determined to be an artist, then he should study in Paris. So Camille enrolled at the Ecole des Beaux-Arts, the official school. He left, however, and had been working at the Suisse since 1857.

While he was at the Suisse, Monet also enjoyed the delights of life in

Paris, which was then the art capital of the world. He went often to the Brasserie des Martyrs, a bar-restaurant near his room in the Place Pigalle, where painters, journalists, and poets gathered to talk about art. A battle raged at that time between followers of Eugène Delacroix, the Romantic rebel against the classical tradition in art, and those who liked the work of Jean Auguste Dominique Ingres, a neoclassicist conservative and the most widely admired French painter of his day. The supporters of Ingres believed that line was more important than color; Delacroix's group felt color was everything.

This life in Paris ended abruptly. In the spring of 1861, Monet had to sign up for the military draft. In France at that time, the draft worked like a lottery. If you drew an unlucky number, you were drafted for seven years of military service. Monet's draw was unlucky. However, it was possible at the time to buy your way out of military duty by paying a substitute to take your place. Monet's father offered to buy his son out of the army if he would give up painting and come back to Le Havre and work in the family business. Monet refused.

He joined a unit called the Zouaves, the African Light Infantry, which was based in Algeria and wore dashing uniforms—boots and spurs, wide pantaloons, a broad sash, a long coat with gold braid, and a little garrison cap. With his hair cut, dressed in the exotic uniform, and longing for adventure, Monet left Paris on June 10, 1861. The desert landscape and the violent sunshine, so different from France, excited him. Every day he saw something new. "The impressions of light and color I received there contained the germ of my future work," he said later.

After a little more than a year in Africa, Monet caught typhoid fever and was sent home to France on six months' leave. In Le Havre in the summer of 1862 he worked hard at painting out-of-doors. By chance he met Johan Barthold Jongkind, a Dutch painter who was staying at Honfleur, the little town across the bay from Le Havre. Monet liked tall, lanky Jongkind, with his thick, disheveled hair and clear blue eyes, and the two painted together often.

Like Boudin, Jongkind painted nature out-of-doors. Monet called Jongkind his second master. "It is to him I owe the final education of my eye," he said later. Monet also developed an interest in making more than one view of the same subject at different times. He would explore this idea more than any other painter of his day.

Still taking an interest in her nephew's art education, Marie-Jeanne Lecadre worried about Monet's devotion to Jongkind and Boudin. She wrote to her friend the painter Armand Gautier that Monet's sketches always looked like rough drafts and that his finished paintings were appalling daubs. Gautier wrote back that Monet should return to Paris at once. When Monet's six months of convalescence came to an end, his aunt, who had seen how hard Claude worked at his painting, decided to buy out the rest of his military term. His father promised him an allowance — if Monet behaved himself, worked diligently, and enrolled in a proper studio under a well-known master in Paris. Monet agreed.

The family turned for advice to Auguste Toulmouche, a fairly prominent painter distantly related to them, and asked him to oversee Monet's education and send regular reports of his progress to Le Havre. In November 1862, Monet left again for Paris. He went to see Toulmouche, who asked him to paint something for him. Toulmouche looked at Monet's small still life. "It's good," said Toulmouche, "but you need discipline to channel your talent. You must go to Gleyre; Gleyre is the master of us all. He will teach you to make a picture."

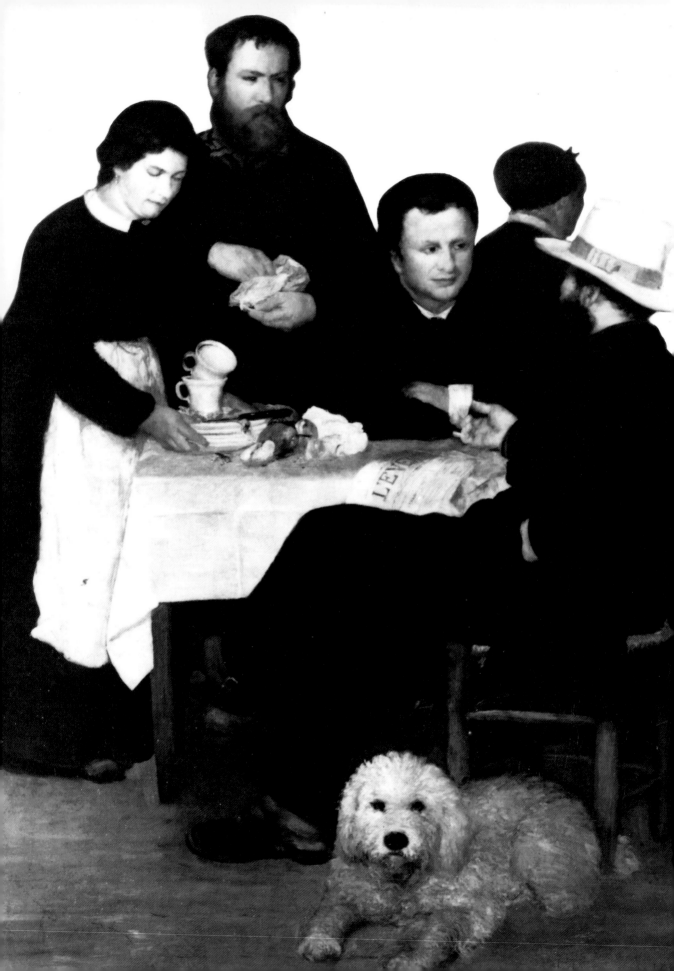

2

NO MORE SCHOOL

Marc Charles Gabriel Gleyre, a Swiss-born artist, was the most lenient of the independent art teachers. In his studio, thirty or forty students drew or painted from a nude model (a man one week, a woman the next) every day but Sunday. Gleyre believed firmly that students should learn to draw before they painted, and when they painted he believed that they should use dark, sober colors. He disapproved of flashy, colorful work. He did not charge his pupils for his advice but asked each student to contribute ten francs a month to pay the rent and the model.

Monet went to Gleyre's studio, set up his easel, and worked for a week on a study of a nude model. The next Monday, when Gleyre made the rounds of his students to criticize their work, he came to Monet, sat down, and looked closely at the drawing. He leaned his head to one side and said softly, "Not bad. Not bad at all. But it's too much like the

1866
Auguste Renoir. MOTHER ANTHONY'S INN
Monet's friend Renoir pictured this group of his fellow artists at the inn where they often gathered for a meal when painting near Fountainebleau. Monet, now fully bearded at the age of twenty-six, stands at the rear; Alfred Sisley, wearing a hat, faces Jules Le Coeur, a wealthy painter who lived nearby. Le Coeur's dog, Toto, waits patiently as the waitress, Nana, clears the table. Mother Anthony herself is seen just leaving the room.

model. He's short and thickset and you have
made him short and thickset.
He has big feet and
you have painted
him with big
feet." Monet
should make

the picture better-looking than the model,
Gleyre said. Nature was all right to study,
but it wasn't interesting. Figures in
paintings should be
beautiful, he said.

1865

THE BODMER OAK, FONTAINEBLEAU FOREST

In his painting of a famous old tree at Fontainebleau, Monet begins to show interest in capturing the precise look and feel of sunlight reflected on the colors of nature. See how much more alive this painting seems than the one of the farm on the previous page.

About 1864

Previous page: A FARM IN NORMANDY (detail)

This rural scene was one of Monet's early landscape subjects.

Monet did not agree. Jongkind and Boudin had taught him to paint what he saw. He was sure that they were right and that Gleyre was wrong. Although he was not happy with Gleyre's instruction or the crowded and noisy atmosphere of the studio,

Monet attended often enough so his father would not cut off his allowance.

It was a good thing he stayed, because there he forged friendships with three students, Frédéric Bazille, Pierre Auguste Renoir, and Alfred Sisley, who would become his painting companions, his allies and supporters for life.

Frédéric Bazille was a tall, handsome young man from a wealthy family in Montpellier in the south of France. His parents, who wanted their son to be a doctor, paid for his art schooling on condition that he continue to attend medical school.

Auguste Renoir, blond and rosy-cheeked, had started work when he was thirteen years old painting china in a factory at Limoges and saved enough money to come to Paris to study art. He was twenty-one, a year younger than Monet, when he started at Gleyre's.

Alfred Sisley, whose father was an English silk merchant living in Paris, was one of the lucky painters to be encouraged and supported by his parents.

Monet told them about the open-air painting techniques he had learned from Boudin and Jongkind. All of them were interested in landscape painting, but only Monet was interested in nothing else. When Renoir persuaded Monet to come with him to copy pictures at the Louvre, the great national museum in Paris, Monet would look at nothing but the landscapes. He was astonished by the much-admired paintings of Venetian canals by Canaletto—the boats had no reflections in the water, he pointed out. That wasn't the way it was in nature, or the way to paint, he said.

Monet and Bazille spent the Easter holidays of 1863 in Chailly, a little village near the Forest of Fontainebleau. The forest had attracted a group of painters, including Daubigny, who stayed at Barbizon, another nearby village. Bazille and Monet set out each morning to walk the two miles to the forest carrying their easels, canvases, and paint boxes. Monet was excited to be in the countryside again. Never mind that only Daubigny among the Barbizon painters finished his pictures out-of-doors and that the others made sketches in the forest but finished paintings in the studio.

Monet stayed on at Chailly after Bazille went back to Paris, causing Toulmouche, the Monet family representative in Paris, to scold him for giving up his studies. Monet replied that he had not given up, he just found a thousand charming things he could not resist.

The jury for the Salon of 1863 was especially severe that year, accepting only 2,217 works out of the 5,000 submitted. Artists complained so much that the emperor himself went to the Palais de l'Industrie and asked to see some of the rejected canvases. They looked no worse to him than the pictures hanging in the Salon so he decided to let the public be the jury. He ordered all the rejected paintings to be exhibited in another part of the exhibition hall, in rooms that came to be called the "Salon des Refusés" (Salon of the Rejected).

Crowds at the exhibition grew larger that year and it seemed that far more people went to see the exhibition of rejected work. When Monet, Sisley, and Bazille visited the Salon des Refusés that spring, they were awed by Edouard Manet's *Luncheon on the Grass (Le Déjeuner sur l'Herbe)*, a painting that shocked Paris. The public thought it vulgar and the emperor himself pronounced it immodest. Manet's brilliant technique and his daring choice of subject matter — a picnic with two women, one of them nude, and two fully clothed men — thrilled Monet and his friends. They talked about Manet's radical color contrasts, the absence of slick brushwork, the lack of dark underpainting, and the way he formed his shadows with colors.

Monet's formal training in painting ended rather abruptly in 1864, when Gleyre decided to close his studio. Monet was relieved. From Boudin and Jongkind, he had learned to use his eyes and he was through with teachers. He went back to Le Havre. There, Aunt Lecadre and his father worried about him because he had sold nothing

1865

When Monet injured his leg while working at Fontainebleau, his friend Frédéric Bazille came to visit. Bazille amused them both by painting Monet in bed, showing the bucket contraption that had been rigged up to keep his wound moist while it healed.

1865

THE MOUTH OF THE SEINE AT HONFLEUR
*Boats, wind on water, sun, sky, and clouds were
subjects enough for Monet: here he paints the harbor across
from his hometown of Le Havre.*

since his caricatures. They complained that he spent too much time in the country and not enough time in the studio. He should either make money, they said, or study under another teacher. Monet, enthusiastic about his work, ignored them. "Each day I discover more beautiful things," he wrote to Bazille.

On his return to Paris, Monet's career exploded like fireworks in a brilliant brief success. He submitted two seascapes he had done in Normandy to the Salon of 1865; both were accepted. Newspapers praised his work. One critic said Monet's two pictures were unquestionably the best seascapes in the show. Another spoke of his "bold way of seeing things," but added that his pictures lacked the finish that can come "only after long study." Finish! Fashion demanded that the picture surface have a finish as smooth as glass and that all brush-strokes be invisible. Critics would say the same thing about Monet for years: He has talent, but things come too easily for him; he must settle down and learn how to paint "finished" pictures. Monet, of course, thought that the life and freshness, the truth of the moment, which he captured in his pictures, was better than any "finish."

More glory came when the souvenir album of the exhibition included a drawing of one of his paintings along with more flattering comments. He sold both paintings for 300 francs each (about $900 in today's dollars). It was quite a start for a twenty-four-year-old painter. The praise and money pleased Monet and calmed his family's anxiety.

Encouraged by his success, Monet conceived an ambitious new project. He planned to paint a huge picture—fifteen by twenty feet, almost as big as Couture's *Romans of the Decadence*—but he wanted to make it a scene of everyday life. Inspired by Manet's *Luncheon on the Grass* of 1863, he decided to picture twelve people at a picnic and paint it out-of-doors in natural light against a real background. It was a revolutionary idea. No painter had attempted a painting of that size and complexity out-of-doors.

Monet went to Chailly to work on the picture, but he needed models and wrote several times to Bazille, who was still in Paris, urging him to come and pose. "If my painting does not work out," Monet wrote him, "I believe I will go crazy." Bazille headed for Chailly. Alfred Sisley also came down to pose with Bazille. Gustave Courbet, a well-known realist who was painting in Barbizon, heard about the enormous picture and came over to Chailly to look at it. He, too, helped Monet by posing.

But Monet had difficulties with the picture. The canvas was so big and hard to move that he had to break his own rule, doing sketches outdoors but working on the painting in the studio. At the end of the summer he took the canvas back to Paris and worked on it, but he could not finish it.

The deadline for the 1866 Salon drew near and Monet was anxious to have an entry. In only four days, he painted a picture of a life-sized woman looking back over her shoulder, her green-and-black striped skirt falling in rich, luminous folds behind her. His model was Camille-Léonie Doncieux, daughter of a well-off retired merchant who had recently moved from the town of Lyons to Paris and lived near Monet's studio. Nineteen years old, Camille was beautiful. She had black hair, white skin, and long black eyelashes. *The Woman in the Green Dress* was accepted by the Salon and won rave reviews.

Instead of being pleased with Monet's second success at the Salon, his family was outraged. They had learned from Armand Gautier that Monet was living with Camille without marrying her. Monet's father ordered him to break with her. When the young artist refused, his father stopped his allowance.

1865–66

Fragment of LUNCHEON ON THE GRASS

The large painting of a picnic that Monet intended for the Salon of 1866 was later left behind in a house where he couldn't pay his rent. The painting was rolled up for storage and it was six years before Monet could recover it. By then water had leaked onto the canvas and rotted parts of it. The central section shown here is one of two parts that were undamaged; Monet threw the rest away.

3

HARD TIMES

Up to this point, Monet's life had gone pretty much the way he wanted. He had not won a grant from the city of Le Havre, but he had gone to Paris all the same. He had studied in his own way and had painted what he wanted to paint. But now at the age of twenty-five, he found himself with no money and the future looking grim.

To get away from creditors, Monet and Camille went to Ville d'Avray, near St. Cloud, west of Paris. In the garden of his rented home, he began work on another big painting — about eight by seven feet, not as big as *Luncheon on the Grass*. It would show four women among trees and flowering bushes, and Camille would pose for all four figures. Monet was determined to paint all of this picture outdoors, on the spot. At first it seemed impossible, since the canvas was so tall. He solved the problem by digging a trench among the flower beds so he could lower the canvas when he wanted to paint the top part. Courbet came by to see him one day and asked Monet why he wasn't working. Monet said the sun wasn't shining. "You could always work on the background," Courbet said. Monet replied that even the background had to be painted in sunlight.

1866

WOMEN IN THE GARDEN

Monet was not very interested in the faces of his subjects and he usually left them indistinct. More important to him was the foliage, the light, and the feeling of space and air around the figures.

Monet and Camille had to move again because they could not pay the rent. Forced to leave several painted canvases behind, Monet slashed them to keep them from being sold. He took *Women in the Garden* with him, though, and continued to work on it after settling in Le Havre. He had hoped to introduce Camille to his father and aunt and win them over, but they refused to meet Camille. She must be an immoral woman, they said. When Monet ran out of money to buy canvases, he asked Bazille to send him the pictures he had left in Paris so he could scrape them, clean them, and reuse them.

To help Monet out, Bazille bought *Women in the Garden* for 2,500 francs, agreeing to pay him 50 francs a month. But Bazille often forgot to send the money, and Monet would become frantic. His troubles were multiplied when he learned that Camille was pregnant. Then the jury for the Salon of 1867 rejected *Women in the Garden*. The Salon had accepted his seascapes and his portrait of Camille — they met the standards of the day — but the new picture, painted in dappled sunlight, struck them as strange and unsuitable. It was Monet's first rejection.

Now desperate for money, Monet appealed to his father, who refused to help him unless he gave up Camille. The elder Monet also told his son not to distress his aunt with news of his predicament, even though Adolphe also had a mistress who had just given birth to a baby. Meanwhile, Camille grew paler, and Monet wrote Bazille that he barely had strength to hold his brushes.

1867
THE CRADLE (detail)
Monet painted his infant son, Jean, being looked after by Camille.

1867

TERRACE AT SAINTE-ADRESSE

Monet painted the tidy garden of his aunt's summer house at Sainte-Adresse, near Le Havre. His father (in the straw hat) and his aunt appear in this painting.

To get money to pay for a nurse for Camille and the necessities for her and the baby, expected that summer, Monet decided to pretend to give in to his family. He took Camille to Paris in April 1867, managed to sell two pictures, and gave the money to Camille. He went back to Le Havre, promising to send Camille every franc he could get his hands on and also promising to acknowledge the child as his. He spent the summer dependent on his family, writing to Bazille, begging him to send money so that he could be with Camille when the baby was born.

Monet began to have terrible headaches and the doctor told him to give up painting in the open air. This terrified him. He quarreled with his father and stayed with his aunt at her summer home in Sainte-Adresse. During a spell of cloudy weather, he was able to paint outdoors again and he worked like a madman, covering twenty canvases with figures, landscapes, and seascapes, including one of the boat races at Le Havre. "Everybody admires every stroke of my brush," he wrote to Bazille. If it weren't for the approaching birth of the baby, he said, he would be totally happy. He longed to be in Paris when the child was born and again and again he asked Bazille to send money.

Monet was not with Camille when his son, Jean-Armand-Claude Monet, "a big, beautiful boy," was born on August 8, 1867, but Madame Lecadre took pity on him and gave him the money for train fare to Paris, where he painted a picture of Jean in his cradle. But he could not afford to stay very long with Camille and Jean and went back to Le Havre to paint.

When he sold *The Woman in the Green Dress* for 800 francs, he returned to Paris and he and Camille and the baby lived in a small room near the Rue Batignolles. On New Year's Day 1868, they were without any heat and Monet, desperate, appealed to Bazille again. Bazille bought a still life.

At the Salon of 1868, Monet managed to get one painting, *The Jetty at Le Havre*, accepted, thanks to the efforts of Daubigny, who was on the jury. Monet heard later that it had been extremely difficult. The newspapers praised Monet's picture, but he sold nothing and once more was out of money.

Monet took Camille and Jean to the countryside and began to paint. When he couldn't pay the rent, his landlady threw him out ("as naked as a worm," he wrote to a friend), keeping his clothes, canvases, paints, and brushes. Monet wrote to Bazille to ask for immediate help and told him he had found a place where Camille and "my poor little Jean" could stay for a few days. He planned to leave for Le Havre that night to try to get something out of an art patron.

The art patron in Le Havre was a rich businessman, Louis-Joachim Gaudibert, who was interested in his work. Monet painted portraits of him and his wife; Gaudibert bought two of Monet's seascapes and gave him an allowance for a while. The money bought Monet and his family a brief period of financial security. He rented a cottage at Fécamp, a little town on the coast north of Le Havre. When the Gaudibert portraits were finished, he joined Camille and Jean there.

This newspaper illustration from Monet's time shows La Grenouillère — a small island in the Seine River, the floating restaurant, swimmers, and all the details of the several paintings that he and Renoir created there in 1869.

Monet was happy at Fécamp and said he was surrounded by everything he loved. He spent his time on the beach or in the countryside, which he thought was perhaps more beautiful in winter than in summer. "And then in the evening, dear friend, I find a good fire and a nice little family in my cottage," he wrote to Bazille, telling him how sweet Jean was. He did not envy Bazille in Paris. Whatever he did at Fécamp would at least not look like anyone else's work. And then he used a prophetic phrase: "It will just be the expression of what I shall have felt, I, all alone," he said.

He did go back to Paris, however, and worked in Bazille's studio on two paintings for the Salon of 1869. They were rejected. Monet kept on. He was experimenting with light and shadows, and, like Manet, using colors instead of black paint for shadows. He saw color

in the atmosphere; even snow reflected color. But how could he capture that light with pigment? He decided to stop mixing colors on his palette and began to apply pure colors directly to the canvas. If he wanted to create orange, for example, he put a brushstroke of pure red on the canvas next to a stroke of

1869
Auguste Renoir. LA GRENOUILLÈRE

1869

*Renoir's view of the riverside
resort (opposite) shows the island
and a corner of the restaurant;
Monet's view is from the
restaurant looking toward the shore
and pictures the boats and one
of the bridges to the island.*

pure yellow. The eye of the person looking at the picture blended the red and yellow and saw it as orange.

Renoir was interested in the same techniques and the two artists decided to work beside the Seine River that summer. Monet found lodgings in a cottage near Bougival on the Seine near Paris. Renoir stayed with his parents not far away, near Louveciennes, where Pissarro and his wife and children lived.

Monet had pleasant surroundings, congenial friends, and exciting work—but no money. "For eight days we have had no bread, no wine, no kitchen fire, no light," he wrote Bazille, urging him to send money. Renoir brought bread from his mother's table to Monet and his family to keep them from starving.

Renoir, almost as broke as Monet, wrote to

Bazille when he had the money to buy a stamp and told him that he was nearly always at Monet's. "One eats nothing for days," he wrote, "only I am happy all the same because, for the painting, Monet is good company. I do almost nothing because I don't have many colors." He said it was Monet who kept his spirits up that summer.

Monet was, indeed, in good spirits, and what kept him most enthusiastic was that he had a subject for a big, new painting. "I have a dream," Monet told Bazille, when he wrote again to ask for money, "a painting of the riverside resort at La Grenouillère." Renoir, he reported, also wanted to paint the scene.

La Grenouillère was a floating restaurant in the Seine built on a large raft with a canopy for a roof. Pontoons connected it to the riverbank and to a tiny island, called "the Camembert" because it looked like a round Camembert cheese. Working-class Parisians came out on the train, spent the day, and enjoyed the sunshine and the fresh air.

La Grenouillère was the perfect place for Monet to paint at that moment. He was interested in real subjects of daily life, and here were ordinary people enjoying themselves out-of-doors. He was interested in the landscape in natural light, and here the light was marvelous: sunshine flickered through the leaves and sparkled off the water, reflecting the trees and the people; drops of glittering water cascaded from splashing oars. Renoir and Monet painted very similar views of the happy scene at La Grenouillère. They used small dots and dashes of pure color to catch the flickering vibrations of light on water, the spontaneity of the action, and the giddy joy of the scene.

When he went out to paint, Monet once said, he tried to forget what it was he saw — a tree, a house, or a field. He simply thought, "Here is a square of blue, here an oblong of pink, here a streak of yellow," and painted it just as it looked to him, until it matched his own fresh impression of the scene. He once said that he wished he had been born blind and then had suddenly gained his sight so that he could begin to paint this way without knowing what the objects were that he saw before him.

Monet's joy in his work was not matched by any improvement in his financial condition. He wrote again to Bazille for money and stressed that he needed it desperately. In September 1869 Bazille suggested that Monet find some sort of work more lucrative than painting. "If I were in your place," Bazille said, "I would chop wood."

Monet was not amused. He could not work because he had no paints. He felt jealous of painters who had enough money for supplies and the jealousy made him feel guilty and angry at everyone. And there was no hope at the Salon. The 1870 jury rejected his

1868

THE RIVER

In this painting of Camille on a bank of the Seine at Bennecourt, Monet has begun to use the dots and dashes of pure color that will characterize what are now called "Impressionist" works.

pictures, while accepting the work of his friends Renoir, Sisley, Bazille, and Pissarro. "And Monet is the greatest of us all," Bazille wrote to his parents. It was no comfort to know that Daubigny and Corot both resigned from the jury to protest the rejection of Monet's canvases.

4

"THESE IMPRESSIONISTS!"

Camille's parents made it known in 1870 that all would be well between them and their daughter if Monet and Camille would marry. They would even help support little Jean. "It's not the most cheerful prospect," Bazille said, "but the child must eat."

The wedding took place in Paris in the summer of 1870. Monet's father, who never forgave Camille or even met her, was not present. Nor was his Aunt Lecadre, who was eighty years old and ill. (In fact, Monet's aunt died not long after the ceremony.) The newlyweds and Jean went to the seaside at Trouville. Boudin and his wife were there and the two families spent time together on the beach, the men sketching, the women talking and playing with Jean.

The serenity at the seaside did not extend to Paris. In July, Napoleon III formally declared war on Prussia, France's old enemy to the east. In Le Havre one day, Monet heard rumors of a new draft and a possible invasion and saw people crowding on board ships for England. Fearing that he might be called into the army, he quickly went to England, leaving Camille and Jean to follow.

While Monet painted in the London parks, at Westminster, and at the docks, the Prussians were winning the war. Paris was surrounded and food was in short supply; people were forced to eat cats, dogs, and rats. France finally admitted defeat when Paris surrendered to the invading Prussians on January 28, 1871.

In London, Monet ran into Pissarro, who gave him news — and it was bad. Bazille had joined the army and been killed in battle. Renoir was in a cavalry regiment, Boudin in Brussels. Pissarro also told Monet that the house in Louveciennes where Monet had stored a group of paintings had been turned by the Prussians into a butcher shop. The fate of the paintings was uncertain.

Monet also met Daubigny in London, and the older painter introduced him to Paul Durand-Ruel. One of the few art dealers in Paris, Durand-

Ruel had left his gallery on the Rue Laffitte and opened one in London. "Here is a man who will be stronger than us all," Daubigny told Durand-Ruel. The dealer was Monet's savior; he bought a number of pictures for three hundred francs apiece.

In January 1871, Monet's father died. Monet's inheritance was much smaller than he had expected, because shortly before he died, Adolphe Monet had married his mistress, Amande Vatine, and legitimized their daughter, Marie. Amande and Marie received the bulk of the estate.

1870
THE BEACH AT TROUVILLE
Grains of sand are still stuck in the pigments of this sketch that Monet made on the beach at Trouville, where he worked beside his old friend Boudin.

Back in France all was chaos, as the empire fell and the country endured the rise and fall of several governments. With money from Durand-Ruel, Monet went to Holland with his family in May 1871. They settled at Zaandam, near Amsterdam, for the summer. While he painted canals, tulips, and windmills, Camille gave French lessons to people in the town.

In addition to finding many interesting scenes to paint in Zaandam, Monet made a discovery that would profoundly influence his work. The story goes that he came home from the grocery store one day and found that the paper wrapped around his purchases was actually a work

1873

MONET'S HOUSE AT ARGENTEUIL

*The house that Monet rented for his family in the Paris suburb of
Argenteuil had a garden for little Jean to play in. Here, like all small
boys at the time, Jean wears a dress.*

of art, a Japanese wood-block print in brilliant colors. Monet went back
to the store, where he found more prints. He happily bought them all,
to the grocer's astonishment. Thus began Monet's own collection of
Japanese prints. He had seen them before, and had been struck by their
bright colors, the strong diagonal lines in their composition, the
strange perspective — to French eyes — the absence of shadows, and

1874

Edouard Manet. THE MONET FAMILY IN THEIR GARDEN
*Monet's friend Edouard Manet came to visit one day and
painted the family.*

the way some figures were cut off abruptly by the edge of the page.

Monet returned to France in the fall of 1871 and gathered as much of the work he had left behind as he could find, some from the family of Bazille and a few surviving canvases from Pissarro's house in Louveciennes. Following his instinct to be near water, he rented a little house in Argenteuil, a picturesque small town on the river Seine only fifteen minutes by train from Paris.

Monet worked hard at Argenteuil. He painted forty-six pictures the first year he lived there, almost as many as he painted during the three years at Bougival, Trouville, London, and Holland. When he put together a sum of money he bought a bargelike boat and built a blue-green cabin on it to make a floating studio like one of Daubigny's. One of Monet's neighbors, Gustave Caillebotte, was a painter himself and also a marine engineer. When he saw Monet building his cabin, he offered his expert help. Interested in boats, pictures, and gardening, the two became friends. Caillebotte even began to buy pictures.

France prospered in the first postwar years. Durand-Ruel, the dealer Monet had met in London, came back to Paris in 1872 and again bought pictures from Monet. Monet briefly knew real prosperity; in 1873, his income was 25,000 francs. Monet began to feel more confident about himself and his future and the confidence seemed to show in his work. The pictures he made at Argenteuil—the river, Camille sewing, Jean playing—reflect happiness and peace.

Early in 1874, Durand-Ruel, feeling a pinch as the postwar boom ended, was forced to stop buying pictures. Money once again became a problem for Monet.

If they were ever to make any money with their painting, Monet thought he and his friends should put on their own exhibitions, independent of the Salon. The four landscape painters Monet, Renoir, Pissarro, and Sisley had much in common with Paul Cézanne, a painter-friend of Pissarro, Berthe Morisot, a young woman pupil of Manet's who was serious about painting out-of-doors, and to a lesser extent with Edgar Degas, who was not interested in landscape. All of them disliked history painting and looked for subjects drawn from contemporary life. They all believed freshness and spontaneity should be preserved in a finished painting, even if people said it looked "sketchy." And, since the Salon so often rejected their work, they agreed that they needed to find a way to show what they were doing so buyers would know about it. (Monet had not sent anything to the Salon since he was rejected in 1870.)

In 1874 they staged their exhibition. Thirty artists opened their show in the large rooms of a photographer's studio in Paris on April 15, 1874, two weeks before the official Salon opened. On the first day 175 people came, compared with the thousands that flocked to the Salon each day, and during the rest of the month attendance held steady at a little less than 100 a day. Few pictures were sold.

Nearly everyone who came was bewildered by the pictures of

1874
Edouard Manet. MONET IN HIS PAINTING BOAT

landscapes and everyday life with their rough surfaces and patches of brilliant color. Many people thought the artists were poorly trained and anxious to get attention any way they could. Some visitors found the pictures puzzling, while others thought them the work of lunatics. An early visitor to the show announced merrily that the painters had discovered a simple way to fill their pictures — they loaded a gun with paint and fired it at the canvas. The joke was repeated all over Paris. Though some reviewers admired what they saw for its freshness and freedom, others called it a "highly comical exhibition" and one critic singled out Monet's paintings as "the most absurd daubs in that laughable collection of absurdities." "Monsieur Monet," wrote one critic, "seems to have declared war on beauty."

1873
Auguste Renoir.
MONET PAINTING IN HIS GARDEN AT ARGENTEUIL
Renoir came to visit and painted Monet painting.

The show had one positive result — it gave the group of painters their name. One of Monet's paintings of Le Havre, showing two small boats leaving the harbor as a red sun rises in the mist enveloping the sea and the sky, still lacked a title. Just as the catalogue was going into print Monet said, "Put 'Impression' on it."

Critics pounced on the word "impression" and mocked it. "What is this picture?" Louis Leroy asked of Monet's newly titled *Impression,*

Sunrise. "*Impression*—I was certain of it. . . . Wallpaper in the process of being manufactured is more finished than that landscape." Another critic dismissed the group of painters with contempt as "These Impressionists!" For years Monet and his friends had talked about how important the artist's instantaneous *impression* was to landscape painting. Now it was official; they were *Impressionist* painters.

Pissarro, Renoir, and Monet were bitterly disappointed with the outcome of the show. They all needed money. Pissarro had to move his family in with his wife's parents. Sisley, whose father had lost all his money in the war, was now as poor as the rest. Monet, undaunted, tried to encourage them all when they visited him at Argenteuil that summer.

1873–74
LE BOULEVARD DES CAPUCINES
Although most of his work was done in the country, Monet painted many Paris scenes, especially of the busy and colorful life of the city streets, often seen from a high vantage point.

Monet and his friends persisted in holding their own exhibitions even when later shows were received with as little enthusiasm as that first one. An auction in 1875 of works by Monet, Renoir, Sisley, and Morisot resulted in actual violence. The auctioneer had to call the police to keep people from tearing the canvases with canes and umbrellas. "We had

1872

IMPRESSION, SUNRISE

This is the painting that gave the Impressionist movement its name.
Monet's view of the foggy harbor of Le Havre as the sun comes up was
shown in the first group show that he and his friends organized.

good fun with the purple landscapes, red flowers, black rivers, yellow and green women, and blue children that the popes of the new school have brought to the admiring public," wrote one critic. Among the few pictures that sold, some went for less than their frames were worth. Monet received 4,665 francs for twenty pictures, an average of 233 francs, but the auction money was not enough to support him and his family; he turned to every friend he had, asking for small loans.

5

WEATHERING THE STORM

As Monet faced yet another money crisis in the fall of 1876, when Camille was ill, an art collector named Ernest Hoschedé came to his rescue. Hoschedé and his wife, Alice, had inherited money, a share of a Paris department store, and a château southeast of Paris. What was more important, Hoschedé admired the Impressionists and had bought their paintings. He invited Monet to come to the château

Alice Hoschedé posed for her portrait on a horse in a photographer's studio.

and paint panels to decorate a room there. But Monet had no money for paints and brushes, so Hoschedé advanced him part of his fee so he could buy what he needed.

Life at the château was luxurious. Special trains brought visitors from Paris. Guests were entertained lavishly and waited on by many servants. In spite of the luxury around him, Monet worked hard while he was there and found that painting the large panels was exciting. He did views of the pond, the garden, the hunt, and a flock of white turkeys that roamed the grounds.

Finishing work at the château, Monet set out for Paris to begin working on a new series of pictures. He had chosen an urban setting this time, the Gare Saint-Lazare, the station where the trains from Rouen and Le Havre arrived in Paris. Monet was fascinated with trains, which were still fairly new in France. He spent days at his easel in the station painting the steam from the heavy locomotives, the bold-colored signals, the crowds, the trains arriving and departing, and the sky seen through the glass roof of the station. Somehow, Monet impressed the stationmaster, who would actually reschedule trains so Monet could finish a picture; he would order engineers to blow white smoke so Monet had a good effect.

Of the twelve Saint-Lazare paintings that he completed, Monet showed six at the Impressionist exhibition in 1877. Visitors were shocked. One very rich collector hurried to the door, shouting angrily that he wanted his admission money returned. A critic said that Monet was trying to make his viewers feel the way travelers did when they heard several locomotives blow their whistles at the same time. He sold few works.

Financially, 1877 was a disastrous year for Monet. He took in 15,197 francs for pictures, but saw little profit. For instance, he sold 10 paintings to one dealer for a total of 1,000 francs. He traded sixteen canvases to a paint dealer to clear his bill and received in cash only 50 francs. His expenses were high—he had to keep up the household at Argenteuil and owed rent on a studio in Paris. Camille was pregnant again and ill. He appealed constantly to friends and fellow artists for help, saying, truthfully, that he would be on the street, that all his furniture was going to be sold, or that his landlord would seize his pictures if he did not receive 200 francs immediately. Deciding to economize, he gave up the house in Argenteuil and moved to Paris, somehow managing to keep his family together.

1877

LA GARE SAINT-LAZARE—
THE TRAIN FROM NORMANDY

Railroads were still quite new in Monet's time and they fascinated many painters, with their puffing steam engines, their sleekly painted cars, and the big, bustling, glass-roofed steel stations in cities. Here, Monet captures the excitement and energy of the Gare Saint-Lazare, where the trains from his old hometown in Normandy entered Paris.

There was bad financial news elsewhere. In the spring of 1878, Ernest Hoschedé was forced into bankruptcy and lost everything. Even the château, which belonged to Alice, was mortgaged and claimed by creditors. All of Hoschedé's Impressionist paintings had to be sold. The poor man first tried to commit suicide, then fled to Belgium. Alice, who was pregnant, started out with her five children for Biarritz so she could stay with her sister. On the way, Alice went into labor and the train was stopped for the delivery. She gave birth to her sixth child, Jean-Pierre, in a compartment on the train while a stationmaster entertained the five

other Hoschedé children. Afterward, Alice returned to Paris with the children and lived in a small apartment, sewing for others and giving music lessons.

The Monet family was in unhappy circumstances as well. After Monet's second son, Michel, was born, in March 1878, Camille was in worse health than ever. Edouard Manet went to see the Monets and found his friend "absolutely on the rocks and in despair." Monet asked Manet to find somebody who would buy ten or twenty pictures at 100 francs apiece. Manet could not, but he put up the money himself to tide Monet over.

1875
WOMAN WITH A PARASOL
Monet painted Camille and Jean out for a walk. Here, he was clearly interested in the challenge of showing them against the sun. See how a halo of light outlines the figures and how Monet fills the shadows with color rather than painting them as flat, dark areas.

With Manet's help, Monet found a house farther down the Seine, in Vétheuil, where rents were cheaper. When their furniture was loaded on the moving van, Monet had no money to pay the movers and had to appeal to his friend the novelist Emile Zola, for help. To complicate matters, all eight members of the Hoschedé family, including Ernest, who had returned from Belgium, joined the Monets in the small house in Vétheuil. Nobody had any money.

Monet worked desperately hard but made only 450 francs in August and 460 in September. October was a little better because he began to sell some of the landscapes he had painted around Vétheuil. The two families moved to a larger house, which had steep steps that led down to the river. They raised rabbits and chickens to eat. But in November Monet received only ten francs for his work. Hoschedé was supposed to pay two-thirds of the household costs, but he failed time and time again to come up with his share of the money and, instead, ran up bills in the neighborhood.

The winter of 1878–79 broke records for cold weather, and snow was still deep on the ground in mid-April. Camille and her baby were always sick. Alice Hoschedé, who nursed Camille faithfully, tried to earn money by giving piano lessons. Monet's friend Caillebotte saved them all from starvation several times by advancing substantial sums of money. Monet sent twenty-nine pictures to the fourth Impressionist exhibition that spring (commenting on his rough brushwork, a reviewer wrote that Monet must have painted all of them in one afternoon). He was delighted when Mary Cassatt, an American Impressionist painter, bought one of his pictures for $300.

Monet went to Paris to try to sell pictures to get enough money to pay the pharmacist and Camille's doctor. He was totally unsuccessful, and, in fact, had a hard time raising the railroad fare back to Vétheuil. He could not paint. The publisher Georges Charpentier and a baker named Eugène Murer had advanced him money for paintings he was to do for them and they hounded him to deliver the pictures. He put up as security for a loan everything they owned, including a locket that Camille had managed to keep during all the years of poverty.

Worst of all, Camille was dying of cancer and in terrible pain. Her suffering oppressed them all.

1875
Sketch for
WOMAN WITH A PARASOL
Monet seldom made drawings before painting, but for this work he did a preliminary study, perhaps because of the unusual perspective and lighting.

Finally, emaciated and in agony but still conscious, she died on September 5, 1879. Watching her on her deathbed, Monet noticed the changes in color that death brought to her face and decided to paint a last picture of her. He told a friend that while he painted he was aware of the lack of emotion he felt as his painter's eye observed the light on her face and calculated which paints to use. This was, after all, the woman he had chosen for his wife, the mother of his children. He was a slave to his art, he said, unable to be free even at a time that should arouse intense emotion.

The winter that followed was as bitter as the one before it; the Seine froze solid. All eight children were sick. Money troubles continued. The laundress, when she did not get paid, kept all their sheets. Caillebotte advanced another considerable sum and Monet's brother Léon sent 40 francs. Household expenses swallowed it up. Life seemed as bleak as the frozen river.

Monet painted many pictures of the Seine that winter. The thaw that followed the freeze was frightening, for ice floes swept down the Seine, causing damage to buildings along the banks.

Monet sketched his son Michel with Jean-Pierre Hoschedé, who would become his stepson.

Monet was thankful that their house was high enough to be out of danger and that his studio-boat, which he had brought from Argenteuil, escaped serious damage. His pictures of the breakup of the frozen river, full of gloomy grays and rusty purples, seem to reflect his despair. In an attempt to earn more money, he put many of these paintings up for sale. Critics said they seemed even more unfinished than his usual work. Even his friends said Monet was exhausted by too hasty production.

Monet at about the age of thirty-five.

Monet decided to try for the Salon again in 1880, the first time in ten years. His decision horrified his Impressionist friends, but he felt that he had to do anything he possibly could that might help him bring in more money. He submitted two pictures; the judges accepted only one and then hung it so high it could hardly be seen. He never tried to enter the official exhibition again.

He had better luck when *La Vie Moderne*, a new weekly review devoted to art and literature, sponsored in its editorial offices the first one-man art shows in Paris. Monet's work was shown right after the Salon, and it was in connection with this that a writer from *La Vie Moderne* came to Vétheuil to interview the painter.

"Where is your studio, Monsieur Monet?" asked the reporter.

"My studio!" said Monet. "I never had a studio. This is my studio!" With a theatrical gesture, he waved his hand toward the hills of Vétheuil and the Seine below.

Admission to the *La Vie Moderne* show was free and people crowded to see it. Some were indifferent; some laughed; few understood what the artist was trying to do. Monet's work still shocked. But the critics were less unfriendly. "Claude Monet is the one artist since Corot who has brought inventiveness and originality into landscape painting," the critic and collector Théodore Duret wrote.

Monet's fortunes improved when Durand-Ruel found backing from a bank and was able to reopen his gallery in 1881. Since some seascapes Monet had painted the summer before had sold well, Durand-Ruel financed a trip to Etretat, on the coast near Le Havre. During his stay on the shore, Monet decided that he would paint a storm at sea. He found a hollow in the cliff where he could plant his easel and lashed it down with strong cords. Fastening his canvas to the easel, he began painting as the rain began to fall. The water rose in pounding breakers. The storm worsened. Monet ignored it, painting furiously. Suddenly, an enormous wave tore him from his perch. Choking underwater, he saved himself from being swept away by letting go of his palette and brushes and grabbing the rope that held his easel. Two fishermen who happened to be on the cliff rescued him.

Monet took a group of the Etretat pictures to Durand-Ruel, who advanced him 2,000 francs and paid his paint dealer 500 francs. Back at Vétheuil, Monet recuperated, exhausted but reassured of the future.

In 1881 Monet decided to move to Poissy, a town nearer Paris where there was a good school for Jean. Alice Hoschedé decided to go with Monet. Until this moment, she had been able to explain her position in the household by saying that she had stayed at Vétheuil to nurse Camille and to help care for Jean and Michel Monet. Her abandonment of Ernest Hoschedé and move to Poissy was considered scandalous, but she simply said that Monet's boys needed her.

Monet never liked Poissy and insisted he could not work there at all—the light and the landscape were all wrong, he said. He made 31,241 francs during the year 1882, the most he had made in many years. In the winter of 1882–83, as the lease was about to expire on the Poissy house, the Seine flooded. The first floor was underwater, and the house could be reached only by boat. Monet determined to find a place where he could finally settle down to paint.

1883

ROUGH SEA—ETRETAT

The high, rocky cliffs, stony beaches, and rough seas
of the Normandy coast attracted Monet for several years
because he was interested in dramatic settings.
Here, the turmoil of the waves, the patterns of the cliff,
and the thatch-roofed old hulls sheltering nets
add up to a dynamic result.

6
GIVERNY

In the spring of 1883, Monet began to search up and down the Seine valley for a house to rent. One day he went to Vernon, about forty miles northwest of Paris, and took the little train that ran along the Epte River. The train was slow; it stopped everywhere. Apple trees were in bloom and the meadows were brilliant with wild flowers.

One of the villages along the way was Giverny, a quiet spot lying between the Seine valley and hills covered with vineyards and apple orchards. There, beside the main road, Monet found a big farmhouse to rent, with two acres of garden and orchard. It was a high, rambling house with pink walls, a slate roof, gray shutters, and at each end a low barn with a dirt floor. A big, walled French country garden laid out geometrically with box-wood, flower beds, and an *allée*—a broad central walk bordered with cypress and spruce—ran down to the railway. On the other side of the tracks was the Ru, a small river that flows into the Epte, which flows into the Seine. Across the Ru were marshes full of aquatic plants, bordered by willows and lines of tall poplars, and, a few miles beyond, the Seine itself. Monet could moor his boats on the Seine and, best of all, the light changed constantly over the gentle land along the valley. "Once settled, I hope to

1885–90

IN THE WOODS AT GIVERNY—BLANCHE HOSCHEDÉ
AT HER EASEL WITH SUZANNE HOSCHEDÉ READING
Monet returned to a motif similar to his early Women in the Garden,
when he painted his stepdaughters Blanche and Suzanne, at left.

produce masterpieces," he wrote to Durand-Ruel, "because I like the countryside very much."

With an advance of money from Durand-Ruel, Monet moved the family and their furniture to Giverny. He took one of the dirt-floored barns for his studio and put in large windows. He began at once to plant a vegetable garden in order to have vegetables for the table and a flower garden so he would have flowers with which to paint still-life pictures on rainy days. The garden, sloping gently south to the valley of the Seine, was warm and sunny. He dug up the spruce and cypress, clipped boxwood bushes, and planted roses that climbed on metal arches over the *allée*. He filled the flower beds, which lay in straight rows, with bulbs, annuals, and perennials so that flowers were always blooming from spring to autumn, carefully arranged according to colors.

Monet brought from Vétheuil four boats — the studio-boat, a row-boat, and two mahogany skiffs — and moored them at l'Ile aux Orties (Nettle Island), a small island at the mouth of the Epte. A favorite expedition for the whole family was the walk to Nettle Island through the cultivated fields.

During school holidays, the whole family joined Monet on his painting trips. Some of the children painted; others played. Alice sewed. In warm weather they went swimming from the studio-boat; Monet was often the first to dive off the cabin roof into the Seine. In winter the shallow water in the marsh froze and they ice-skated. In the spring the whole family went mushroom hunting.

Life was good at Giverny. Monet, now middle-aged, was still a big, handsome man with a brown beard and bright eyes. Alice was charming and gregarious, a good hostess, and an intelligent admirer of Monet's work. Monet treated all the children as though they were his own, and

1891
HAYSTACK IN WINTER
Monet's long series of paintings in the fields near his home
show his obsession with the specific effects of light on natural forms.

1894
ROUEN CATHEDRAL,
THE FACADE,
MORNING EFFECT

1894
ROUEN CATHEDRAL,
WEST FACADE

*In nearly every one of Monet's paintings of the cathedral at
Rouen the carved stone of the facade seems almost to dissolve in
a shimmer of color. Neither the architecture of the building nor the
spiritual nature of the place interest him. He is trying to capture
the feel of the atmosphere in each moment.*

1891

Right:

POPLARS ON
THE BANK OF
THE EPTE

1891

Left:

THE POPLARS

*Most of Monet's pictures
of the trees along the Epte
River are vertical in format,
like the one at left,
probably because he was
seeing the poplars from near
water level and wanted to
emphasize their height.
In a few cases, however,
he used a horizontal
canvas and came in closer
to their bases to stress
the long line in which
they grew.*

everyone—Alice, servants, children—called him Monet. Hoschedé died in 1891 and the following year Monet married Alice. The two of them and the eight children lived on as before.

Monet got up every morning at four or five o'clock and studied the sky. If it was rainy, he went back to bed; if it was fair, he stayed up. After a big breakfast, and often accompanied by Alice's daughter Blanche, he would start out into the countryside wearing a beret and wooden shoes like the ones the local farmers wore, pushing his painting equipment in a wheelbarrow. He came back home at eleven o'clock for lunch, a cup of coffee in the studio, and perhaps a glass of plum brandy. If the light was still good, he went out again to paint. Dinner was at seven.

Monet thrived in the happy routine of Giverny, but he had a terrible temper, which could be set off by an unexpected visitor, a mishap in the kitchen, or bad weather. (When he was in a temper about his work, the children were very quiet at mealtimes.) Eventually, Alice would jolly him out of his sulks.

He was quite unforgiving about his work. He destroyed hundreds of pictures, burning as many as thirty canvases at a time. Once, in a fit of anger, he kicked his foot through a painting of his stepdaughter Suzanne standing on a hill. Regretting his hasty action, he had the canvas neatly mended. Another time, frustrated while in his studio-boat, he decided to give up painting forever and threw his paints, palette, and brushes into the river. The next day he wanted to work, but it was Sunday and no paint store was open. He wired Paris and an obliging dealer went to his store and selected supplies for Monet,

1891

Opposite: HAYSTACK, WINTER, GIVERNY

sending them to Giverny by the next train.

For a long time, Monet believed that he should finish pictures on the spot, outdoors, but as he grew older he did more and more reworking. Once an American woman bought a painting of Etretat in his studio. Monet told her that he wanted to do something to the sky before he delivered the painting as the clouds did not quite suit him. It might take a little time, he explained, because he would have to return to Etretat and wait for a day when the sky and atmosphere were virtually the same as they had been when the painting was started.

Although there was much in Giverny and the valley of the Seine to paint, Monet also loved to travel, looking for new *motifs*, or subjects, and atmospheric effects. He went to Venice, Norway, London, Brittany, the south of France. In May 1889, he visited the Creuse valley and began painting an oak tree still bare from the winter. As the weather grew warmer, leaves appeared on the tree. Monet was upset that his motif was spoiled, and he offered the tree's owner 50 francs to have all the leaves removed. It took two men to bring ladders tall enough for the job, but Monet was able to finish his winter landscape in May.

Motif and effect were the two issues that concerned Monet the most when he painted. Throughout his working life he searched for the motif—a road, a riverbank, a bridge, a group of trees—that would stimulate him to capture its form and light with color. Reflections and silhouettes appealed to him. He chose his motifs with care, and always painted what he saw, never composing an imaginary landscape with elements from other places. Monet worked at a painting only as long as an effect lasted—rain, clouds, snow, sun, fog at dawn, or twilight.

In the autumn of 1890, Monet stayed home in Giverny to work on what became a large series of paintings, among them some of his best-known and best-loved works. These were pictures of *meules*, stacks of grains such as wheat and oats, which have a shape quite different from haystacks. Monet claimed that he had a moment of miraculous inspiration one day as he was painting the stacks. The light changed suddenly and he asked Blanche to fetch him another canvas. As time passed and the light changed again, he asked her for more canvases. He would work on each canvas a few minutes—as long as the effect lasted—and then start another. He returned the next day to work on the same canvases, switching them on his easel as the light changed. After that, he always worked on two or three canvases at once, returning to the same place day after day to wait for the return of a particular effect. He painted the *meules* at different times of day and under different conditions of light and weather—in the calm of afternoon, in late evening when the hillside was blue, on cloudy days when the trees in the distance looked like ghosts, and in midwinter when they were covered with snow. Eventually he would complete them all, picturing the most fleeting effect in detail. And from this idea grew his passion for creating series of paintings, works devoted to one motif that expanded the visual possibilities far beyond that of a single painting.

In 1891 Monet did twenty-five paintings of a field of poppies at Giverny and then began work on a series of pictures of poplar trees. He would take the studio-boat up the river to where a row of poplars grew along a curve of the Epte. From the river, he painted the trees as he saw them and reflected in the water. He worked fast. Sometimes, he said, he would have only seven minutes to paint the sunlight on one leaf. The town of Limetz decided to sell one particular stand of poplars for lumber. But Monet wasn't finished painting them, so he went to the timber dealer who wanted the trees and asked how high a price the man expected to pay. Monet promised to make up the difference if the auction price went over this amount, on condition that the trees would be left standing for a few more months so he could finish painting them. The timber dealer agreed.

Monet's next series was of the facade of the great Gothic cathedral at Rouen, an important city on the Seine. In 1893 he went to Rouen and found a place where he could paint on the second floor of a building directly opposite the cathedral. But the room was part of a millinery shop, and Monet's work space was the area where women tried on hats. When the customers objected to his presence, Monet built a small enclosure in which he could work at the window unseen.

He painted the cathedral's carved stone facade in mists that turned the surface to lace; he pictured it in sunshine, trying to catch the changing effects of the light on the surface and on the colors of the building from hour to hour. He described how the sun's rays slowly dissolved the mist that clung to the rough stone, creating an *enveloppe* of vapor around it. The *enveloppe* (a

Theodore Butler, an American artist who came to Giverny to be near Monet and later married his stepdaughter Suzanne, made this drawing in 1890. Notice that Monet is wearing sabots, *the wooden clogs worn by French farm workers.*

French word meaning, roughly, the colored light that surrounds objects and brings them to life) was crucial to Monet's painting.

By the late 1880s, the persistence of the Impressionist painters in exhibiting their work bore fruit. The public accepted Impressionism. Monet's money troubles were over. (Durand-Ruel sold twenty of the Rouen paintings for as much as 15,000 francs each.) When his landlord decided to sell the Giverny house in 1890, Monet was able to buy it. He built a new studio in the garden and his old barn-studio, which had been given a wooden floor, became the family's sitting room.

Once again Monet set out to improve the gardens. The chalk subsoil was near the surface of his flower beds, and he enriched them with imported earth. He subscribed to gardening magazines, sought advice from his friends, hired gardeners, imported exotic plants, built greenhouses, and devised elaborate planting schemes. He built more trellises for roses against the walls of the house. He planted Virginia creeper and clematis. The garden grew famous. He bought another plot in the village where he could grow vegetables, leaving all the beds at the house for flowers.

Monet became a celebrity, and as the years went by painters of many nationalities were drawn to Giverny. In 1887 the proprietress of the village grocery store and her family moved out of their house so they could rent rooms to visiting foreign artists. Some of them — Theodore Robinson, for example, an American Impressionist painter who became a friend of Monet's — eventually bought houses in Giverny. At one time, forty American artists were working in Giverny, so many that Madame Baudy's grocery store began to sell paints and canvases. Monet ignored most of the American painters. When they asked his advice, he told them to "look at nature."

7

THE WATER LILIES

In 1893 Monet bought a parcel of land beyond the railway line. On this plot, the river Ru formed a small pond, where wild arrowhead and water lilies grew. Monet planted new hybrid strains of water lilies and built a bridge over the pond, copying its design from Japanese prints that he admired.

Eight years later, Monet bought more land so he could make the pond bigger. To do this, he had to dig ditches to bring water from the river Epte. The farmers and laundresses who used the stream were afraid that Monet might cut off their water supply or that his exotic plants might poison the cattle downstream, but he finally won permission from the town council of Giverny to enlarge the pond. Monet filled the new pond, which was four times as big as the old one, with water lilies. He trained wisteria on an arched trellis on the bridge, which now crossed a small arm of the bigger pond. The scene was set for Monet's last great drama, his battle to paint the water and the water lilies bathed in light and air.

Monet first painted a picture of the small pond in 1892. By 1900, he had painted his new, bigger pond twenty times. In 1902 he began working on a long series of studies of water lilies and reflections in the water. He was in his sixties and conscious of the passing of time. He had to deal with declining strength, occasional dizziness, and bouts of

Monet in his study at Giverny.

Monet, eighty years old, shows a visitor
to Giverny some of his paintings, including one
of the remaining fragments of the large
picnic scene that he was unable to
finish in time for the Salon in 1866.

depression. He was having trouble with his eyes. But he painted on.

Durand-Ruel exhibited forty-eight of these paintings in his gallery in 1909 under the collective title *Les Nymphées: Paysages d'Eau (The Water Lilies: Water Landscape)*. They seemed unlike any paintings viewers had seen before. All the critics praised them, and one described them as upside-down landscapes. The panels seemed to belong together, and people who saw them said it was a shame to break the series up. Monet had already decided he wanted to decorate a circular room, which would be completely filled with a painting of water and flowers.

About 1916
WHITE AND YELLOW
WATER LILIES
Many water-lily paintings fill the canvas, with objects seen close and no horizon line, immersing the viewer in a lush, private world.

Alice became ill with leukemia in the spring of 1910 and doctors held out no hope for a cure. She died a year later in May 1911. The house seemed desolate and empty. That summer Monet, seventy years old, found out he had cataracts on his eyes; the lenses had become clouded, altering his vision. At arm's length—the usual distance for painting—his sense of color was inaccurate. Although surgery was not necessary immediately, Monet was in despair. He finally began to paint again and returned to the water-lily decorations. Just before World War I began, in 1914, he started building still another studio, this one large enough to hold the panels that he had in mind. (Some of his water-lily paintings were almost fifteen feet long.) Work, he said, was the great consolation.

From 1914 until his death, in 1926, he struggled to paint the water lilies. He painted indoors on the longest panels, working from sketches made outdoors. He did the narrow panels outdoors. In spite of his age, his eyesight, and his temper, he was incredibly productive.

Visitors loved the paintings. In them, it seemed that water and sky had no beginning and no end. "It was as though we were present at one of the first hours of the birth of the world. It was mysterious, poetic, deliciously unreal," the art dealer René Gimpel wrote.

By 1918 Monet had finished thirty large canvases, but he would sell none of them. On November 11, 1918, the day that World War I officially ended in victory for France and her allies over Germany, Monet wrote to his old friend Clemenceau, who was now premier of France, that he wanted to give two panels to the nation to celebrate the victory. Clemenceau came to see Monet and asked him to donate the whole project to the country. Monet agreed to give the nation twelve *Water Lily* panels if they would be hung in a special building where the viewer could see them all around him.

It took a great deal of negotiating to work out an agreement between the French government and Monet

1899
WATER LILIES
AND JAPANESE BRIDGE
The dense blooming of flowers and water lilies seen in paintings and in photographs of Giverny often make the place seem overgrown, but Monet's plantings were carefully organized and tended.

on a building suitable for the *Water Lilies*. Monet insisted that the panels be hung in a circle or an oval, not in straight lines. The government refused to build a special building because of the cost. Finally, Clemenceau came up with the idea of using the Orangerie, an empty building near the Louvre Museum that had once housed the orange trees grown for the Tuileries Palace in Paris. Monet said he would sign nothing until he was satisfied that the Orangerie could be remodeled to form a circular or oval space. If the state would furnish the proper space, he would give eighteen panels instead of twelve.

Everyone finally agreed on the choice of two large connecting

1919
THE PATH THROUGH
THE IRISES
Although water lilies were Monet's favorite flowers, he grew nearly every kind. A visitor once described a visit to his gardens as "entering a paradise. It is the colorful and fragrant kingdom of flowers."

oval rooms on the lower level of the Orangerie, and in the spring of 1922 Monet signed a contract. His paintings would line the walls and the government agreed that nothing else would ever be exhibited there.

As 1922 went by, Monet's eyesight worsened. He wasn't sure what his work really looked like. During the summer, he burned and cut many canvases. Years earlier Paul Cézanne had said, "Monet is only an eye, but, my God, what an eye!" And now that eye was failing him. He finally agreed to have an operation. In 1923 the first of two operations

JAPANESE BRIDGE AT GIVERNY

The simple Japanese bridge in the water-lily garden was designed by Monet as a visual element rather than as a necessity. He painted it often.

on one eye was successful enough that he could see the odd things he had been doing with his paintings before the operation. A second operation on the same eye helped still more, but he began to have trouble perceiving colors. Sometimes everything looked blue, other times yellow. Glasses sometimes made things better, sometimes worse. The doctor was unable to explain what was happening. Monet destroyed more paintings. Clemenceau urged patience. Monet replied he would rather be blind than go through such anguish.

By September things were better. Monet reported his near sight was almost perfect. He could read without difficulty. But there was still trouble with color. At this point, his sight was better when he was close to the canvas, but trouble began when he stepped back a few yards.

Then, miraculously, Monet could paint again. At Christmas 1923, Clemenceau told him that the Orangerie would be ready by Easter. Monet kept repainting the *Water Lilies,* and Clemenceau reminded him that he had made a bargain with France and the government had kept its promises to the letter and at great expense.

A new doctor, Jacques Mawas, prescribed different glasses. In July 1925 Monet said he could see better with one eye than he ever did with two. He still could not part with his *Water Lily* paintings.

During the winter of 1925–26, his health began to fail, and it

Monet, close to eighty years old, poses beside his water-lily garden at Giverny and the Japanese bridge trailing with wisteria.

became apparent that Monet, who had chain-smoked cigarettes most of his life, had lung cancer. He was ill, but not confined to bed until the very last. Clemenceau had lunch with him two weeks before he died. Monet could talk of nothing but his garden and some Japanese lily bulbs that had just arrived. When he died, on December 5, 1926, Clemenceau was at his side.

His funeral was simple, as Monet had requested. There were no speeches and no religious service. The mourners walked in procession from the house to the churchyard in Giverny, where he was buried.

After his death, the *Water Lily* decorations were hung in the Orangerie, Monet's gift to France and to the world. "There is in these waters the reversed reflection of unseen trees, and then at the end one gets a little dizzy and is surprised not to be walking on the ceiling,"

Monet poses in the studio he built for the creation of his Water Lily series.

Gérard d'Houville, a reviewer, wrote of "these somewhat magical portraits of fragile flowers, treacherous waters, changing reflections, rapid hours, and fleeting instants."

Monet had worked all his long life to attain one goal: to paint light and nature as he saw them in one brief moment. With little formal schooling and almost no formal art training, he endured the most wretched poverty, the alienation of his family, and the insults and ridicule of an uncomprehending public. But he accomplished what he set out to do and changed forever the way we see the world.

LIST OF ILLUSTRATIONS

PAGE 50. Edouard Manet. *Monet in His Studio Boat.* 1874. Oil on canvas, 32$^7/_{16}$ × 39$^9/_{16}$". Neue Pinakothek, Munich, Bayerisches Staatsgemäldesammlungen. Photo: Artothek, Joachim Blauel

PAGE 51. Auguste Renoir. *Monet Painting in His Garden at Argenteuil.* 1873. Oil on canvas, 18$^3/_8$" × 23$^1/_2$". Wadsworth Atheneum, Hartford. Bequest of Anne Parrish Titzell

PAGE 52. *Boulevard des Capucines.* 1873–74. Oil on canvas, 31$^3/_4$ × 23$^{13}/_{16}$". The Nelson–Atkins Museum of Art, Kansas City, Missouri. Acquired through the Kenneth A. and Helen F. Spencer Foundation Acquisition Fund. F 72–35

PAGE 54. *Photograph of Mme. Alice Hoschedé on Horseback..* Collection J.M. Toulgouat. Photo: Abrams Archives

PAGES 56–57. *La Gare Saint-Lazare, The Train From Normandy.* 1877. Oil on canvas, 23$^1/_2$ × 31$^7/_8$". The Art Institute of Chicago, Mr. and Mrs. Martin A Ryerson Collection 1933.1158. Photo: © Art Institute of Chicago. All rights reserved

PAGE 58. *Woman With a Parasol.* 1875. Oil on canvas, 39$^3/_8$ × 31$^7/_8$". The National Gallery of Art, Washington, D.C. Bequest of Mr. and Mrs. Paul Mellon

PAGES 1 and 59. *Sketch for Woman With a Parasol.* 1875. Drawing, 21 × 16$^1/_4$". Courtesy Durand-Ruel, Paris

PAGE 60. *Michel Monet and Jean-Pierre Hoschedé.* 1885. Charcoal on canvas, 28$^3/_8$ × 23$^5/_8$". Collection Michel Monet, Giverny. Photo: Abrams Archives

PAGE 61. *Monet at about 35.* Photo: Abrams Archives

PAGE 63. *Rough Sea, Etretat.* c. 1883. Oil on canvas, 25$^5/_8$ × 31$^7/_8$". Musée des Beaux Arts, Lyon. Photo: Georges Kriloff, Lyon

PAGE 65. *In the Woods at Giverny—Blanche Hoschedé Monet at Her Easel with Suzanne Hoschedé Reading.* 1885–1890. Oil on canvas, 36 × 38$^1/_2$". The Los Angeles County Museum of Art, Mr. and Mrs. George Gard De Sylva Collection (Detail on page 64)

PAGE 67. *Haystack in Winter.* 1891. Oil on canvas, 25$^3/_4$ × 36$^3/_8$". Museum of Fine Arts, Boston. Gift of Misses Aimee and Rosamond Lamb in Memory of Mr. and Mrs. Horatio A. Lamb. 1970.253

PAGE 69. *Rouen Cathedral, West Facade.* 1894. Oil on canvas, 39$^1/_2$ × 26". National Gallery of Art, Washington, D.C. Chester Dale Collection, 1963.10.49 (1713)

PAGE 69. *Rouen Cathedral, The Facade, Morning Effect.* 1894. Oil on canvas, 39$^3/_8$ × 25$^5/_8$". Museum Folkwang, Essen, Germany

PAGE 70. *The Poplars.* 1891. Oil on canvas, 39$^3/_8$ × 25$^3/_4$". Private collection. Photo: Michael Tropea, Chicago

PAGES 71–72. *Poplars au Bord de l'Epte.* 1891. Oil on canvas, 34$^3/_4$ × 36$^1/_2$". Private collection. Courtesy Acquavella Gallery, New York

PAGES 73–74. *Haystack, Winter, Giverny.* 1891. Oil on canvas, 25$^5/_8$ × 36$^1/_4$". The Art Institute of Chicago, Mr. and Mrs. Martin A. Ryerson Collection. Photo: © Art Institute of Chicago. All rights reserved

PAGE 78. Theodore Robinson. *Claude Monet, Giverny, 1890.* Drawing after a photograph. Galerie Durand-Ruel, Paris

PAGE 81. *Photograph of Monet at His Desk.* Courtesy of The Bancroft Library, University of California, Berkeley

PAGE 82. *Photograph of Monet in his House at Giverny With the Duke de Trevise in 1920.* Photo: Roger-Viollet, Paris

PAGE 83. *White and Yellow Water Lilies.* 1916. Oil on canvas, 78$^3/_4$ × 78$^3/_4$". Kunstmuseum Winterthur, Gift of the Galerieverein Winterthur, 1952

PAGE 84. *Waterlilies and Japanese Bridge.* 1909. Oil on canvas, 35$^5/_8$ × 35$^5/_{16}$". The Art Museum, Princeton University, from the collection of William Church Osborn, gift of his family (y1972–15). Photo: Clem Fiori

PAGE 85. *The Path Through the Irises.* 1919. Oil on canvas, 78$^3/_4$ × 70$^7/_8$". From the private collection of the Hon. and Mrs. Walter Annenberg

PAGE 86. *Japanese Bridge at Giverny.* 1900. Oil on canvas, 35$^3/_8$ × 39$^6/_{16}$". The Art Institute of Chicago, Mr. and Mrs. Larned Coburn Memorial Collection. 1933–441

PAGE 87. *Photograph of Monet Beside the Japanese Bridge, Giverny.* Photo: Roger-Viollet, Paris

PAGES 88–89. *Photograph of Monet in His Studio at Giverny, 1923* . Photo: Roger-Viollet, Paris

INDEX